The

Content

Code

By Evette Rose

Edition 1

ISBN: 9798875630637

Disclaimer

All information obtained from Evette Rose, or anything written or said by her, is to be taken solely as advisory in nature. Evette Rose and Metaphysical Anatomy™ will not be held personally, legally, or financially liable for any action taken based upon their advice. Evette Rose is not a psychologist or medical professional and is unable to diagnose, prescribe, treat, or cure any ailment. Anyone using the information in this book acknowledges that they have read and understand the details of this disclaimer. Evette can discuss the metaphysical explanations for psychological disorders but are unable to diagnose, prescribe, treat, or claim to cure any illnesses that require medical or psychiatric attention. The principles taught in Metaphysical Anatomy™ and in this book is based on Evette's life experiences and are guidelines and suggestions to support those seeking simple tools to improve their quality of life. By utilizing and using this book, the participant acknowledges that he/she assumes full responsibility for the knowledge gained herein and its application. Material in this book is not intended to replace the advice of a competent healthcare practitioner. The reader takes full responsibility for the way they utilize and exercise the information in this book.

Legal

All recordings and publications obtained from Evette Rose, or this book remain the intellectual property of the aforementioned and must not be used or reprinted in any way without the written permission of Evette Rose. Any unauthorized commercial use of Evette Rose's name, photograph, images, or written material is strictly prohibited and is in direct violation of rights.

ACKNOWLEDGMENTS

Thank you to each and every client or student that I have met for your insight, support, and willingness to share your life stories. I would not have been able to write this book without you! Thank you, Noemi Idang, for your unconditional support!

With Love,

Evette Rose

The Contentment Code

Also by the author

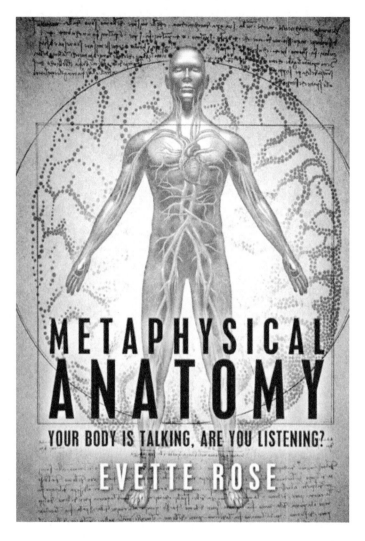

Metaphysical Anatomy is about 679 illnesses from A – Z. This book is so much more than the emotional components of each disease. Metaphysical Anatomy also includes step-by-step guide for identifying the origin of the disease process, whether it be in your ancestry, conception, womb, birth, or childhood. This book is equally valuable for experienced alternative healing practitioners, psychotherapists, hypnotherapists, personal development coaches and those interested in self-healing.

Psychosomatics Of Children
Your Ancestry is talking
Are you Listening?

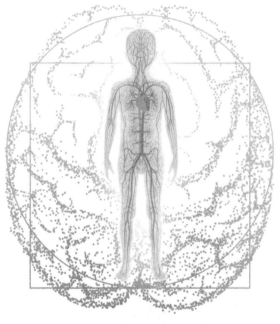

Evette Rose
METAPHYSICAL ANATOMY VOLUME 3

Psychosomatics of children is the sister book of metaphysical anatomy volume one. This book focuses on children's ailments and psychological challenges. Children have not had a full life yet. Therefore, ailments in their bodies are stemming from womb and ancestral trauma, which is unresolved. Not only is your body talking in this book, but your ancestry is talking, are you listening?

DECODING
Trauma

A DIFFERENT PERSPECTIVE ON TRAUMA

Evette Rose

Trauma Decoded. It's time to get back to who you really are! This book is for people who want to change their lives but don't know where to start or what steps to take first, because they have never looked at themselves before, or because they have tried everything else and failed so badly that they feel like a failure and it's easier not to try again than risk failing again, which would make them feel even more of a failure. You are not destined for failure! You are destined for greatness!

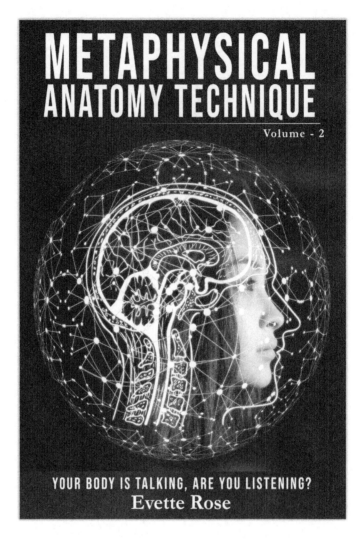

Metaphysical Anatomy Technique Volume 2 explains the core foundation and healing technique behind Metaphysical Anatomy Volume 1 which describes step-by-step guide for identifying the psychosomatic pattern related to 679 medical conditions. These conditions can be activated by circumstances in your present life, your ancestry, conception, womb, birth trauma, childhood, or adult life. Volume 2 teaches you the foundation of Volume 1 including a powerful healing technique. There is also an Online Healing Course that you can combine with Volume 1 and Volume 2.

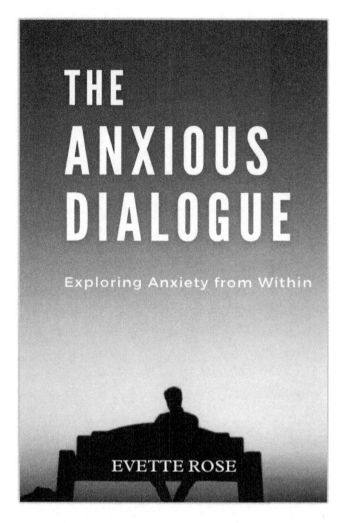

"The Anxious Dialogue" is a self-help book that helps you get unstuck, live with more ease, and feel better. It's a workbook for your mind, heart, and nervous system. It's a quick read with tons of exercises to help you challenge your thinking patterns and change the way you respond to stressors in your life." It has exercises and practical advice that will help you stop your anxiety from controlling your life. You'll learn to identify the patterns and habits that keep your anxiety going, then choose new ways of thinking and behaving to replace them. You'll also be able to practice this new way of being immediately with fun, easy-to-use steps to help you relax and reduce stress.

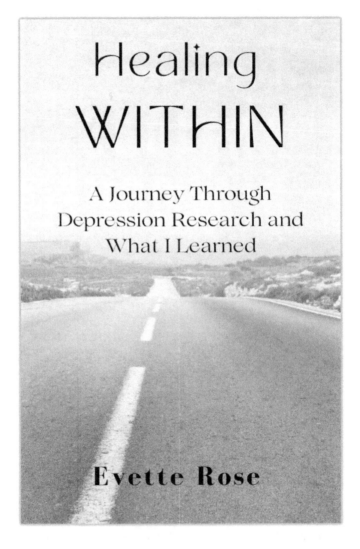

Depression can be a heavy, difficult-to-lift weight. It can sap your energy and make it hard to motivate yourself. But depression is a real condition that often requires treatment. There are many different types of depression, with various causes. Some people experience depression in response to a specific event, while others have ongoing, long-term problems that contribute to their depression. Depression can affect anyone, regardless of age, race, or gender. It's not always easy to recognize, but there are ways to get help.

"The Pain Puzzle" is a book about pain and how to deal with it. Chronic pain affects millions of people worldwide, but there's still so much we don't understand about it. Our goal for this book is to give you the tools you need to understand with your own pain, as well as share some of our findings from research on the topic." If you're suffering from psychosomatic pain, emotional pain, or any other type of ailment pain, "The Pain Puzzle" can help you understand your pain from a new perspective. The Psychosomatics of pain refer to the idea that our thoughts and emotions can contribute to pain. For example, someone who is constantly worrying about their pain may find that their pain gets worse. Our understanding of pain has come a long way, especially in my research. In this book, I will share my research regarding pain, chronic pain, and psychosomatic pain.

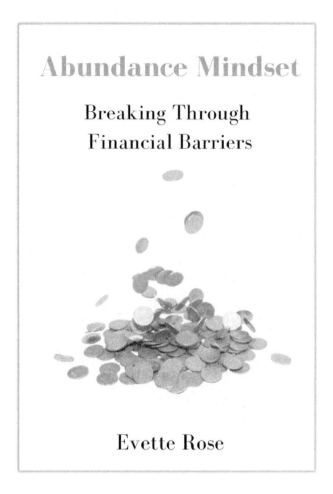

Abundance Mindset

**Breaking Through
Financial Barriers**

Evette Rose

Address your abundance mindset to create prosperity and abundance. Manifest success and heal blocks to abundance with this powerful financial tool. Get clear about your values and ancestry to empower your financial future. Create awareness around your relationship to money for lasting change. This is a great guide to getting your money in order and becoming successful. Get blocks off your energy and start achieving your goals with this helpful guide to financial awareness. Heal your relationship with money and achieve abundance with this valuable guide to financial ancestry. Discover your values and manifest wealth with this enlightening guide to financial success. If you can resolve and release these issues, you will open yourself up to a more prosperous future.

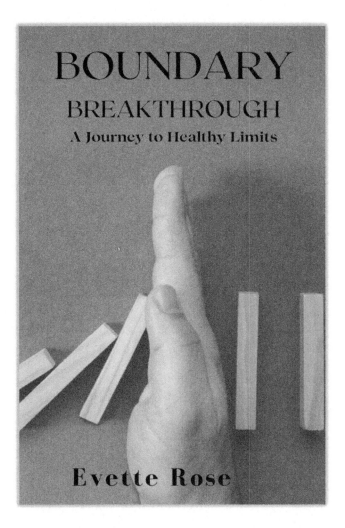

"Boundary Breakthrough" is a self-help book that will help you reclaim your life. It's a guide to understanding and setting healthy boundaries and learning to say no when you need to. If you've ever felt trapped or held back by your relationships, this is the book for you. "It is relatable, and packed with information that will change your life for the better. If you're tired of feeling like you're constantly walking on eggshells, it's time to get your boundaries back! This book will help you set healthy limits and finally start living the life you deserve. build resilience and thrive in the face of adversity, this is the book for you!

"The Content Code" is a life-changing book that will show you how to be happy. It's packed with powerful techniques and strategies that will help you overcome unhappiness and trauma. You'll finally be able to find your purpose in life and achieve your birthright to happiness. This book is engaging, and easy to read - perfect for anyone who wants to start living a happier life today! It's a guide to overcoming trauma and negative associations that hold you back from happiness.

Communication Blocks

A Journey in Understanding
Communication

Evette Rose

"Navigating Communication Blocks" is a communication tool designed to help you become more effective and successful at communicating with others. It is based on the premise that most people have some sort of block when it comes to communicating effectively. By becoming aware of these blocks, you can resolve them and improve the way you communicate with other people. This will lead to better relationships, more success in your career, and greater happiness overall.

"Elevate Yourself" is a book that will help you release your past self-sabotaging patterns, clear out your negative associations with yourself, heal your confidence, and more. This book is all about finding love for yourself, no matter what you've been through. It's about learning to forgive yourself for the things that have happened to you in the past or even recently. It's about letting go of old stories that keep you stuck. It's time to shine your light!

"Embrace the Heartbreak" is a guide for turning your life around after a relationship. It includes exercises that will help you discover the root of your problems and give you tools for moving forward with grace and ease. This book is for anyone who has ever questioned their self-worth or felt lost in love. This is a self-help book that helps you heal from heartbreak, divorce, relationship challenges, and abuse. It shows you how to manifest the love of your life and values into your life. This book helps you change the negative patterns in your life, such as sabotage and regret.

Are you tired of being abused? It's time to break the silence! I can relate because that person used to be me. In this book share my life story, the good the bad and ugly. Being raised in a violent home along with a drug addicted, alcoholic parent trying to navigate my way through what seemed to be the beginning of the end. "Reclaiming Your Inner Light" is here to help you heal from the trauma of abuse and become the confident person you were meant to be.

This true-life story is a must-read for people who have either experienced abuse or care about someone else who may be trapped in processing their childhood experiences. This book brings an empowering message of hope, healing and understanding to anyone who feels challenged by their past.

"Relationship Resolution" is a guide to healing relationships, trauma, anger in relationships and gaslighting. If you're dealing with a narcissist or controlling partner, this book has the solutions you need. Figure out your language for love, boundaries, dating, marriage, and more. Learn about the language of love and boundaries so that you can communicate effectively with anyone in your life. "Relationship Resolution" provides tools to help you heal from narcissistic abuse by learning how to recognize gaslighting. This book will also help you understand abuse and control games in your relationships. It will teach you how to set boundaries, communicate effectively, and love yourself.

Transform
Everyday

Healing quotes and daily journaling

Evette Rose

The healing intention of this book is to create awareness of your blocks and patterns. It is through awareness that healing, and transformation takes place. In this book you will find quotes and inspirations designed to heal and transform every day of the year.

Table of Contents

Getting started

Hi, my name is Evette Rose and welcome to my world. I look forward to starting this journey with you to dive deep into challenges that you might be having in your life. Congratulations for taking active steps to improve your quality of life it takes courage to make a decision, but it takes determination to follow through on the decision that you made. Know that during this journey you are exactly where you need to be.

I invite you to move through this book with ease and with grace with an open mind.

I would love to stay in touch with you and you can join me on any of my events I always have weekly free master classes and free mini workshops.

You can join me on social media hang out have fun and enjoy a tremendous amount of free content that I also share.

Find me at: www.evetterose.com

Free MAT Membership site: www.matmembers.com

Free Masterclasses: www.matmasterclass.com

Introduction

Are you happy on Mondays? Normally, Monday isn't our happiest day. We even call it blue Monday! Everything just seems to go wrong on a Monday. Everyone's still trying to get out of weekend mode.

I know even those people who love going to school or doing their work find Monday an exasperating experience. We all have that Monday blues and stress - so you're not alone.

It's not the best way to start the day when we wake up feeling all overwhelmed and anxious at the start of the week. It's challenging to shift from the weekend's fun and relaxing activities to study mode. Sometimes it seems like the only way we can find happiness is by pushing through Mondays. It's the most challenging day to look for happiness. But here's the thing. What if it's not about finding it? What if it's an experience, an experience to be felt through every fiber of your body? Happiness is taking place all around us, but we cannot fully connect to the experience.

Happiness is always there. It's around you, it's in you, and it's with you every step of the way. It's just a matter of how. How can you plug into the happiness grid and feel the electrical jolts running through your body, veins, and your consciousness?

Happiness is right there with you. Yes, it is here around us. It can even be in the sunshine, in that phone call with your friend, and even in the person's smile beside you. Happiness is a beautiful thought in your mind and a gift that your heart can truly possess.

Most of the time, happiness is there with us, even if we're not aware of it. It's everywhere - throughout each moment in our lives, wherever we are, and whatever we do. It's something that we feel and have within, and it can be addicting. Once we experience genuine happiness, we want more of it.

All the information, all the experiences, everything, held in the quantum field. It's just a matter of whether we are a frequency match to these pieces of information all around us and within us. If you don't have an awareness of happiness in your life, then how can you align with something that you don't recognize? How can you align with it? It starts with taking away challenges, things that have been causing you pain or discomfort. Things that have been diverting you, switching your focus somewhere else. Your focus is everywhere except for things around you that could make you happy if only you could allow it.

While not everyone is fortunate enough to experience happiness so easily, there is no need to worry. No matter what your situation is, there's always a space for happiness in your life. So, open your heart, let happiness in, and enjoy the electrical jolts it brings. Sounds easy, right? It used to upset me when people said that to me. It felt like such a far fetched conception.

Everything in life is a journey. Life itself is a journey. Then you get high-jacked into different directions, emotions, and experiences.

Chapter 1

The happiness conundrum

They say happiness is our choice, not the product of circumstance or something that just happens. Our brains are the most powerful tool we have in this world. This means that we have this power within us to choose how we feel in most cases. We can choose to accept, ignore, or even change it. It's even harder when circumstances trigger deep wounds from the past or even cause new wounds.

Then it's challenging to see the forest from the trees. Keep in mind, I am not referring to real serious conditions when someone has medical reasons for unhappiness (referring to depression). If that is the case, then head over to "Healing Within" book. There could be valuable sources there.

Happiness isn't an end goal, but a progressive journey. It doesn't just come after going through a rough patch, when you're in love, or when good things are happening. It's also not about being in a specific spot to find your joy. You will not find happiness by being in the right at the right time. Good luck with that.

I must share this because happiness was a journey for me as well. In fact. Especially for me, as I grew up in my life, I honestly didn't think that happiness existed. Cheerful people used to upset me. I thought they were faking it, and sometimes people are faking happiness, but at least they are trying. I was not even going to that extent.

Being happy felt like a sham. It felt like a scam. It was like these people were pretending to be happy. You know, like all these Walt Disney movies with people saying, "oh wonderful, happy ending, happily ever after". Yeah, I heard that is true at the massage therapist, but not in life itself.

It's like these programs and ideas of being happy were implanted as layers into your mind. The concept of happiness is talked about repeatedly. How many people have truly nailed it?

You read about it in books like this one, and you read about happiness as far back as the Bible and ancient texts. So, this must be an experience that exists. People have experienced it all over the world and we feel like we can't have it.

We can't have access to it because maybe it doesn't exist. Maybe it's just made for other people. So maybe there's something wrong with you.

Maybe you feel broken, whatever the reason might be. There's a challenge. How big is the challenge for you, specifically? I don't know, but either way, you are here today because there is slight discomfort in your life. There is a slight misalignment. There's something in your life that you feel that's just not a hundred percent working for you.

We all know the truth that life is full of difficulties. We are always changing and so is our happiness. People and things come and go, and both positive and negative experiences often end in a blink of an eye.

Life can be unpredictable. Sometimes we're feeling great, other times not that much! There will always come a time when you'll get disappointed over what someone commented on or shared on Instagram. Sometimes good things happen too. For example, you have a fantastic conversation with your best friend. You might get a compliment from someone at work. Or finally achieving a goal.

One thing that I realized in my life is my attitude toward happiness, and the concept of happiness determined what my experience was going to be.

What you expect is what you come to match. That's what you subconsciously align with and look for. That is how the Reticular Activating System (RAS) works. The RAS is the part of your brain that filters in people and circumstances, and emotional experiences that will relate to how you feel emotionally. Where your focus is, your emotions and energy will flow. I can't be happy. I don't deserve to be happy. Well, there you go. You just decided that, and therefore, it has become your reality.

I am making this point, as deciding to be happy was the first step in my pursuit of finding happiness. Most things in life happen because you decided to act. That decision is your intention. The steps you take after will make or break your outcome.

A simple statement or even complaint such as, "happiness is for other people" is a decision. So, you decide that happiness is for other people. The universe is like, okay, all right, here we go. That's what you believe. That's what you align yourself with. Even though consciously, of course, that is not what you want. However, you're constantly reinforcing this decision. The universe then just responds.

What I just described there was one of my realizations. It was part of my love-hate relationship with the happiness battle. I felt like I was in a boxing ring, and I've been fighting with happiness. I am sure you thought I would say that I was fighting for happiness. Nah, not exactly, I was fighting against it.

I tried to navigate happiness at every turn. I did everything to move through negative experiences to stay connected to happiness, but it became harder to stay happy when you focus on feeling unhappy and what you do not have in your life.

When life kept throwing things at me that made me feel the opposite of happiness, I wondered if it was even worthwhile to keep working so hard to find happiness.

Sometimes you fight so hard for something, and you fail. Just as you surrender and accept what you can't change, things change. This is where I found myself a few years ago. Tired of the fight, drama, asking all the why's, and getting half-assed answers. Dammit, it was exhausting. Even though I didn't fully have it at this point in my life, I have come around to accepting that happiness is essential to living the life of my dreams. It's a beautiful gift that I can enjoy and should never deny myself.

My happiness started through acceptance of where I am at in my life and remembering that it's my damn right to be happy. I discovered that there were blocks that were holding back my happiness. When I recognized these factors that were stopping me from being happy, it shifted my beliefs and opened me up to a whole new level of revelations as I began to fully embrace the truth. What truth? That fact that happiness was always mine never left me.

I realized my biggest block and challenge was my definition of happiness. That held me back and messed up my idea of what I thought happiness should be. That sabotaged me. These stupid movies and novels paint these picture-perfect ideas of what happiness is, and then you can't achieve it, leaving you feeling like a failure. I failed because I aimed to define my happiness based on fiction, and not reality.

I'm going to ask you a million-dollar question that's going to knock your socks off. That's just going to throw things into perspective, quick, because that's how I work. Now let's go right to the root, the real, juicy stuff of why things are how they are.

What are the blocks?

What is this happening?

Why is it so important to understand these questions?

This is a crucial step in creating what you want with ease and grace. Many people fight for peace, fight for their rights, fight, and fight. Look at what you're projecting with that fight response. It's opposition, anger, and resentment going out into the universe.

The universe then says, "Oh, is that what you want to energize? Okay. I'll create more circumstances." This will make anyone feel unsupported by the universe. The universe doesn't understand wrong or right, yes or no. If it did, this world would've been absolutely perfect. It would enlighten us just by living every day and visualizing food and nourishing our body. It just doesn't work that way. That's not where we're at. That's not how the universe works.

It's important, with intention, to create and establish happiness peacefully and to work toward it with ease and grace. Do you get my drift? You don't have to fight for your happiness because it's your birthright to just have it.

It's your God-given birthright to experience happiness. However, sometimes our past gets in the way. Sometimes certain things that we can't quite remove get in the way. Sometimes people in our life get in the way. Maybe it's our poor boundaries, or it's our low self-esteem that's getting in the way. Maybe it's our fear of rejection.

At the end of the day, know and realize that you can have what you want. You deserve it. It is this platform and mindset on which you create your happiness. My biggest challenge, my biggest block, was my definition of happiness. My definition of happiness didn't work for me.

How can I want something that I cannot feel? How do you even create it? That is how manifesting works. You feel what you want, and then you create it. It's confusing, isn't it? I didn't even know how to look for it. I didn't even know when I even felt it. Is it excitement? Is it nervousness? Is it when I cry and laugh at the same time because I felt traumatized, excited, and exhausted all at once? What is it? What is happiness? That's the biggest challenge that we have. What is it, and what is it not?

Now, at the end of the day, happiness for me was the definition that I created around it. I defined the definition according to my own values and desires. It's a definition that brought me peace, calmness, and a sense of belonging. Why? Those were my most important values. We decide what our happiness is based on our current status and values in life. How can you feel happiness if you don't value it? I repeat, how can you feel happiness if you don't value it?

It's like saying to someone, I want to lose weight. I want to exercise. When you ask that person to name their three highest values in life, it's "my job, my parents, my kids." I didn't hear about health. If it's not on your values list, then your focus will not flow there. Now, we need to explore why your focus is not flowing toward health. Why isn't it a value that is important to you?

What is challenging you? What is holding you back from valuing health? We'll get into that a little further along in the book, but not about health, blah, I meant happiness.

Chapter 2

What stops us from experiencing happiness?

Are we unintentionally blocking our happiness? Do you feel that something is stopping you from being truly happy at this moment? There are painful truths that we have to accept. However, acceptance does not mean defeat. I repeat, acceptance does not mean defeat. Acceptance means you accept what you cannot change. You can't control everything, period.

After all, we are striving for that deep sense of inner peace and knowingness that everything is ok. No matter what, everything is going to be ok. I understand the need to feel safe because I was raised in a home which included an alcoholic, drug addict, and violent father. It was one of my highest values in life. My pursuit of safety in all aspects of life blinded me to value happiness. Happiness didn't make me feel safe, yet I craved it so much. Let's look at those factors so you can be more aware of and more in control to take back your happiness. These points I am sharing are from my happiness journey and the battle I had with it.

You are subconsciously not choosing to be happy

Despite being such a simple sentence, it's challenging to grasp this. According to the Law of Attraction, you attract the things you give the greatest attention to and put your mind into. It becomes tougher to be happy when your thoughts are directed toward all the negative aspects of your life. If you decide to pay attention to the positive and happy aspects of your life, you will see them. Remember the RAS example I shared with you.

You are living in comparison

If you always compare your life to those of your friends, neighbors, family members, or even strangers you meet, then you may frequently judge yourself as less than others. How can you feel worthy if you only focus on what you lack?

When you see everyone having a great time, going over social media photos of your friends living their best life, then you end up seeing yourself as lonely   and you feel fed up. You may frequently view yourself as inferior as everyone else seems to live the good life, but you're not. God bless those friends anyway. May their life truly be as good as it is in social media. This is not true. This creates unfavorable emotions that finding contentment and happiness seems nearly unattainable when, in fact, they are attainable. So, when you find yourself getting caught up in comparison, remind yourself that everyone in this world will shine in their special light.

You subconsciously turn to self-sabotage

The bully inside your mind can be ruthless. Even when things are going well for you, there's this inner critic. There's this strong internal pull that drags you back into misery. It appears there is a part of you that believes you don't deserve to be happy and wants to prove that you are wrong.

You are sabotaging the relationship you have with yourself because you obsessively overthink everything in your thoughts and put so much pressure on yourself to be flawless that you end up ruining your ways of being happy. It's hard work to always try to be perfect. That was my life, and I gave it up. I am who I am wherever I am, period.

You stick to believing in "if only"

Nothing kills your happiness more than thinking that it only exists "out there." Or when you tell yourself, you'll be happy "if only" you have more allowance, get that promotion, feel admired by everyone, drive a new car, buy everything you want, etc. This way of thinking hinders you from being happy and thus out of reach. Believing in "if only" deprives you of the beautiful moment that you are currently experiencing.

You are stuck in the past

Even if there is a lot to be thankful for in the past, it might not make you happy in the future. If you had a traumatic past, then yes, it sucks. I get it. My life was a mess. Rape, sexual abuse, domestic violence, self-abuse, you name it. I get it to my degree of experiencing it. So, I am not preaching here. I don't say this lightly.

The past teaches and helps us grow, but what happened there is not happening now. You can either live in the past or be present in your life. It all comes down to deciding to choose happiness and making it one of your highest values in life.

When you keep on living in the past, you become more regretful. You'll keep thinking of what you could have done differently and how that would have affected your current situation. This only drains you, and it's placing you in the opposite vibe of happiness. Be mindful of the present and trust that what happened in the past has led you to where you are now. It led me to where I am with you right now.

Seeking constant approval and validation

When you lack self-assurance and confidence, you end up chasing after something you may not even want. You allow other people and someone's opinion to dictate your choices. Your happiness depends on whether they approve of who you are and what you're doing. Your happiness is now in someone else's hands. You just lost your power and path toward claiming YOUR happiness. If that person changes or leaves, then they take your happiness with them. Where does that leave you?

If you love seeking approval all the time, then you'll be wasting time and effort on things you don't truly desire. You are chasing reactions and not fulfilling experiences, which can add to your quality of life. You are waiting for another traumatized person to validate you. Let that sink in.

You are surrounded by fear

Our world is filled with stories and news that make us feel powerless, scared, and unhappy. Sometimes, this fear makes us feel terrified of trying new things or reaching for what we truly desire. We fear failing, being rejected, or doing something wrong. This leaves us feeling embarrassed, discouraged, and ashamed. This fear traps us in a lifetime of what-ifs and deprives us of happiness.

You attach happiness outside of yourself

In our consumer-driven world, it has persuaded us to look outside ourselves for happiness when, in reality, it comes from within. We fall into the trap of entrusting others with our happiness, hoping they would do the same for us. We cannot take responsibility for our pleasure and attribute our discontent to external factors. You attach your happiness to material things that you desire and can't have. Instead of having a deep sense of appreciation for the moment, you are blocking yourself from genuine happiness. I did that too. It was most of my life.

You can't accept reality

You always live in denial. You always want to believe that the grass is always greener on the other side. This hinders you from experiencing happiness as you lose the capacity to accept your life right now. Instead, you get stuck in negative emotions, such as hatred, disappointment, and bitterness. These negative emotions can become a person's fuel. Have you noticed how strong you feel when you are upset versus when you are happy? Where are you pulling your power from? Let that sink in too.

You think that happiness solves your problems

Your idea of happiness may deceive you. You may believe that happiness means putting an end to all negative things and protecting yourself against negative situations, negative emotions, and disappointments. That's not the power that happiness holds. Being happy closely borders on being optimistic rather than pessimistic about life. You might have noticed that optimistic people are happier than pessimistic people?

Chapter 3

Pessimistic fart versus optimistic fairy

The understanding of pessimism versus optimism brought me to an eye-opening experience, especially when I observed myself more from the pessimistic versus optimistic standpoint. We behave in a certain way without questioning the mind frame we are in when we act. Even as a child, we just act and react. We are reactive little creatures at that point. We don't really question why we react a certain way to a challenge.

Our outlook and approach to life stem from somewhere. The foundation of that didn't just randomly come together. Events, people, and circumstances influenced the foundation on which we are now building our lives on.

It's common to copy optimistic or pessimistic traits from our parents. How did they show up in moments of crisis? How did they show up when they were angry? How did they show up when they had to solve a problem? How did they show up for you when you needed support in your life? All these actions and reactions set forward a deep pattern in relation to how you are going to show up in your life as well. Especially what your attitude is going to be.

When you look at what your outlook on life is, are you a positive person? Are you a semi-positive person? Are you a negative person? Or are you a semi-negative person? Are you very optimistic? Or are you very pessimistic? This is when I find that people go one or the other way. There are very few people who sit in between.

Now, of course, you might feel a little more optimistic about certain things in life, and others may be more pessimistic. It fluctuates, and the reason for that is that maybe you have more positive experiences with certain people or certain circumstances. Those old experiences and how you approached them in the past can influence how to act in the present moment when you feel challenged with, for example, with the same issue.

If you had a positive experience during a challenging moment, your outlook later in life regarding that experience you had would be positive. Memories that you're storing in relation to that moment are positive. When your subconscious mind dives into old memories, to relate to circumstances currently taking place, it remembers the positive experiences. Then you're going to have a very optimistic approach and view based on something that you're doing which you had a prior past positive experience with. The same applies to the negative experiences resulting in a possibly wearier possible and pessimistic outlook.

When we look at what conventional wisdom tells us, an optimist, for example, is like a glass-half-full sort of person while a pessimist will see the glass as half empty. There's a lot more to optimism than just that. Where you stand on the optimism-pessimism spectrum affects every single aspect of your day and life, including your mental health. You also know when you focus on being negative, you feel more stressed and anxious. The outcome? You are going to be less happy in life. Because you might always feel that whatever you want, or need is always out of your reach.

So, if you are very pessimistic, you dwell on the worst likely explanation for something bad that is happening. Let's say, for example, you failed a project. If you are pessimistic, you might think, "well, I failed this project because maybe I'm stupid." Whereas, if you are optimistic about the same situation, you might say, "well, maybe I failed, because I didn't try hard enough. Next time, I will work harder, and I will do better."

The key message here is that optimists have more positive explanations when things go wrong. That also explains a lot in terms of how a parent acted when you made a mistake. Their reaction toward you during your developing years is fundamentally important in relation to the relationship that you're going to form with that action, challenges, and failure.

When a pessimistic person, turns to the worst-case scenarios about the future, they can spiral into a very destructive, chaotic thinking pattern. A pessimistic mindset can also negatively affect their entire future and life.

The reason for this is that when we dwell on worst-case scenarios all the time, we feel like our future is bleak. These feelings can quickly lead to symptoms of depression. We can have low moods, anxiety, and especially restless behavior.

People who are optimistic hold a positive attitude towards their sense of self, that is positive, and there is a much lower risk of depression, and falling into that state of, "I'm never good enough."

There is a strong link between self-esteem, optimism, and depression. Since the 1960s, schools and parents have had a lot of focus on supporting children's self-esteem. Schools, for example, would ask the children to write reasons they are special.

The highest priority was boosting a child's self-worth. Even though maybe all this wonderful support was there, in this case, verbal support. Then why are so many people still unhappy?

The key message here is that children today, especially from the 80s to 90s, and the early 2000s, have never been more depressed. Rates of depression have been rising across western countries as well since the 1950s. Many people suffer from depression at a young age.

In 1993, a study found nearly a third of American 13-year-olds had depressive symptoms. Why are generations worse, rather than better? The problem also lies in a very important misunderstanding of what self-esteem is.

We're often given the message that our self-esteem is all about how we feel about ourselves. Feelings are also just one aspect of our self-esteem. The more important component here is how we act in life as well.

When we look at genuine optimism and high self-esteem, it's not about teaching a child to feel special or feel happy all the time. It's not about saying how they should act and behave in situations.

You can't tell a child to feel something if they cannot relate to it. As children, we used to be very black-and-white in our approach to life. It is feedback from our environment that alters how we feel in the future regarding our actions and reactions to challenges.

The often asked question is, how do we define optimism? Many people would say it's adapting to positive mantras or visualizing fortunate outcomes. I would say, it's just a lot of fluff. It could also be a lot more about how you think about the causes of events and how you react to them. What is your attitude and mindset after you experience failure? It depends on whether you see the events as permanent or temporary.

If you are pessimistic, you might then believe that terrible events have a permanent effect. It's never going to end. It's just always going to be this way, and there's nothing you can do about it. You might reason those bad things will keep happening in the future. If you are pessimistic and someone has a negative reaction to you, you might say, "they are a terrible person, and I must not be good enough to be respected."

If you are optimistic and someone has a negative reaction to you, you might actually say, "well, this person is in a terrible state today; they are not feeling well." The difference is that the mood is temporary. So, the optimistic person finds it much easier to be hopeful about the future and possible outcomes. This attitude can make a person more resilient to depression and they can be happy in the long term.

So, are you a fairy or a fart?

Chapter 4

What does happiness mean to you?

We're going to unravel this so beautifully. We're going to be happiness ninjas. When you are done, you will have black belts in happiness. You're going to see exactly why, how, and simple this can be when you know the fundamental points. As a starting point, we are going to define what your happiness is.

This means that you know you are happy when you feel, hear, see, or sense _____ in your life. For some of you, this might be the first time in your life that you're clearly defining what your happiness is. Hello, clarity! Hello, clear communication and intentions. Consciously aligning yourself with people and circumstances can give you support in creating happiness.

I once helped a client to establish what her happiness meant to her. Her values were deeply connected to needing to feel free. To have people around her that don't suppress her inspiration. To feel secure, protected, and not feel like anyone can rip that out from under her. A sense of peace that comes from when boundaries are being respected. She didn't want to fight for peace. I helped her to understand what she wanted the most. She was pushing away the most because of the approach she adapted to, in order to gain her happiness.

What is the concept of happiness?

When we look at the concept of happiness, I think it's safe to say that we're all aspiring to become happy, to become alive! When we truly find that happiness within, then it really doesn't matter what's going on in the outside world, because your happiness remains with you.

In a lot of my quotes that I also post on social media, I talk about having this concept of happiness within, and it took me a while to understand the concept because this was also my journey to finding true happiness and defining what it meant for me.

We all have this idea that happiness means having the perfect partner, having the perfect job, or having a bank account that's full of money.

Maybe they're all accurate definitions of happiness because these definitions suit different people with different needs. We all have different unmet needs which are motivating us to find more happiness.

It's important that we find our own definition of what real true happiness is. So, when you discover it and realize its presence within you, you can recognize it.

I couldn't recognize it. I was so focused on loss and the lack of happiness. I was completely blind to the surrounding things that would normally make me happy if only I had been open to receiving this feedback from my environment. Don't ignore negative feelings, but also note when they dominate your focus on your reality.

This is a huge distinction. Being aware of how you feel is one aspect. Being consciously aware of how your negative feelings can control your quality of life is a whole new powerful approach. This awareness is your superpower. It is in that moment of clarity when you can consciously and actively take action to change your thought process.

Have you noticed that when you are upset, sad or when you are in a place of pain, all you see around you is more of how you feel? More people and circumstances show up in your life in a way that triggers your negative state more. It's a disempowering place to be in. This can cause many people to feel they are sinking and rising above how they feel. Ignoring these feelings will not help either. What helped me? Knowing that there was a solution to my challenges gave me the power and hope I needed.

There is an opposite polarity to everything in life. When there is darkness, light also exists. Where there is happiness, sadness can also exist. When there is a problem, there is also a solution.

This doesn't mean that you have to ignore those feelings. You can't simply shove them away and move on to the next thing you want to do - it doesn't work that way. Whether negative or positive, your feelings exist for a reason - and it's there to tell you something about yourself. It sure as hell taught me a lot.

It is normal to be sad, frustrated, excited or happy. Your feelings and emotions, whether good or bad, are all valid. Take whatever you are feeling right now as cues to what actions you need to take to be aligned with the best version of yourself. I can look at my feelings as messages and guides about what I need to change or not about myself.

When you embrace your emotions (meaning you allow them to be there without judgment), you get to be more in tune with your needs. You ask yourself, what do I need at this moment when I feel a certain way? We don't feel the way we feel for no reason. There are reasons for everything in life, and that includes your emotions as well. It is through this that we can experience a deeper sense of appreciation for ourselves and our deepest needs. Your emotions are showing you what you need. If you ignore it, you will always ignore and cut yourself off from what you need in life.

This brings us back to the RAS that I told you about earlier. You need to break the cycle through mindfulness, and conscious awareness and through healing work. When you are in that place of pain, you just see pain. How do you break that cycle? That is all we want but you need to understand a few things about yourself first.

So here is an important point to remember. Thoughts are incredibly important and powerful. You process at least 90,000 thoughts per day, and 75,000 of those thoughts will repeat the next day. If your mindset is negative and you feel unhappy, then that's exactly what you're going to be investing in your tomorrow.

You are laying the foundation for the day after today, the week after the next, and the month after that, because your thought processes will continue to be repeated if you don't consciously and actively intervene.

I understand that talking about breaking cycles is easier said than done. Because if it were that easy, neither of us would be in each other's company right now. I am sharing this because of my journey and cycles, as well as the value that I found in that.

The reason for not getting better from my experience is that we have underlying trauma that's blocking us from feeling and defining happiness. We block ourselves from being open to receiving happiness that we already have in our life.

We can't receive it because we focus our filters on something other than what we really, truly want. We focus on what we resist rather than what we want. It was for me, but dammit, it's true, isn't it? Imagine investing the same amount of energy you used to resist what you don't want into what you do want? Imagine the magnitude? The catch-22 is when we resist aspects we don't like in our lives; it takes energy. It takes energy to build an energetic wall and to keep it away.

So that means the more we build that wall, the more we come in alignment with the very thing that we try to resist. The more you hate feeling down, the more you hate feeling depressed, the more you hate feeling your environment and your family, your friends, your relationship dynamics, the more they're going to bother you.

It's a very frustrating happiness block that I had in my life. I always told myself I would be happy when I had a car or that perfect partner, and so forth. When I have a perfect job, I will be happy. I will be happy when I have that perfect house. What I had to realize in my life was that the more I achieved these happiness goals that I set up for myself, the farther away I would drift from my happiness. I would go back to square one when I would finally achieve them.

When I finally reached the happiness destination that I would set up for myself, I kept going back to feeling unhappy and dissatisfied with my life. It was because the chase for happiness was over. It was a reality check for me at that moment. Because I used the chase for happiness as a way of distracting myself from how unhappy I was. I didn't believe I could have what I wanted. It was a self-fulfilling prophecy.

These programs played out based on subconscious secondary gains stemming from problems I didn't want to deal with. Here, it was the underlying root of trauma that challenged my ability to be and feel happy.

I ended up running in circles, dealing with the symptoms of my unhappiness rather than looking at the root causes of it. Almost like patching up a chronic sore with a band-aid, I created superficial actions that I would take that would make me happy for the short term. Rather, I should have been looking at the deeper root cause of the chronic infection that was there.

The perceived notion of the happiness that I would experience in the future always excited me. The dream of being happy made me happy, but it was not my immediate happiness.

You might consciously go through moments that are happy. Maybe you're going to your friend's wedding. She's so happy and you are there with her. You can't enjoy that moment with her because you're so stuck in the future of when you will have your wedding or perfect outcome.

Who wouldn't be happy to see their best friend so happy? We have all these blocks! That's just an example, but we have all these blocks.

The Contentment Code

Chapter 5

How to stay grounded in the present?

When you read books or articles on meditation or spirituality, you've probably noticed that the idea of living in the present is a common theme. Even if they all make perfect sense, it is still challenging for us to remain in the present.

Most often, we put too much focus on the future. There's nothing wrong with setting goals for the future as long as we don't get too caught up in circumstances beyond our control. While we can plan for the future, we should be ready to make changes when things don't go according to our plans.

We must give our complete attention to the moment if we want to connect more with ourselves and our loved ones. We can't be there for them if we're preoccupied with the past or the future. It's also hard to be entirely in touch with whom we are if we focus on aspects of ourselves that don't exist, such as in the past or future.

Living in the present moment is challenging. We're constantly distracted by things that can take us away from being fully immersed in this reality and living purely. A powerful way I've found that worked for me to feel more at peace within myself (and others) is through practicing mindfulness meditation techniques such as focused breathing exercises.

Consider a time when you feel anxious or worried. Are you focused on something from the past or worried about something that will happen in the future? When you shift your perspective and pay attention to the present, you are more likely to feel centered, content, and at peace. You are much more likely to pay attention to the positive things that are occurring rather than letting them pass by unnoticed or unappreciated.

This means that being present allows you to savor the good things life offers. It's challenging, but when you do that, happiness becomes a lot easier to access. Did you know that there's no wrong or right way of being happy? There's no perfect quote that will nail the definition of what it should look and feel like. You will know when you feel happy, and you will also know when you feel free.

You'll just know what these aspects feel and look like when you experience them. Happiness for me would mean feeling safe in a relationship dynamic. That's because I felt so unsafe. So, when I resolved the traumas associated with safety, my values around happiness changed tremendously.

When you think about your desire to be happy, have you ever considered that apart from happiness, whatever you want the most might also be the biggest block behind your happiness?

Your happiness should never be outside of you

This was my biggest downfall. It was a rude awakening when I realized I could only be as happy as how people and circumstances showed up in my life. People and circumstances fluctuated. My happiness fluctuated constantly. It was never constant. It was never stable. It was never there when I needed to access it because it depended on other people's moods and behavior.

Very little did I realize sometimes I would try to control and manipulate people to stay a certain way for the sake of the emotional attachment I had towards the way they were. It's how I needed them to be so that I could have the experience of happiness that I wanted. This is also where we lose our happiness because the moment the circumstances change, when people change, we try to stop them from changing. This sabotage is, of course, subconscious.

We may try to change ourselves because we're trying to adjust to get them to act and react in a way that we are used to. This means we might lose our sense of self by trying to reconnect back to our happiness again when the source of it is no longer there or the same.

Then we end up being more unhappy. We are back to chasing our tail and we try to chase people that are just not stable in our lives. Talk about unintentionally trapping ourselves back into unhealthy relationships. Sometimes it's not even the relationship that was unhealthy. It was how we attached ourselves to it, along with the motivating reasons.

Here's the thing. You don't have to change yourself and your entire life to please people or to be happy. While there's nothing wrong with wanting to look good but as we live in a society that is so obsessed with appearances, we go overboard with this, and we might think this will make us happy.

When we compare ourselves with others, we forget to appreciate and love ourselves. When we see celebrities on social media, it's easy for us to think that they are perfect (even if they are not). They also have flaws and insecurities. Instead of paying attention to the amazing things about our body and what we can do, we focus on what we don't have.

We never have to change ourselves for someone else, but we can do it on our own for ourselves. If we change for the best, this will allow us to experience new and exciting things, as well as opportunities that are good for us. For instance, learning new skills or working on your inner self can bring about a difference you never thought was possible.

If you always allow gloom to rule over you, you can also try to commit to consciously turning things around. This means working on shifting your perspective and changing your mindset. Remember the awareness I mentioned earlier? When you become aware of a negative thought creeping up, it's important you realize it's just a thought. It's not happening to you. It's an experience you are having. How you react to this internal experience can drastically affect whether your mood will continue to sink or rise above this thought which is influencing you.

Keep things interesting and be open to new experiences. Why not try something you've never tried or learn a new skill?

Often, change refreshes our attitude toward life. It brings a sense of renewed zest and energy. It also allows us to accept different circumstances with an open mind, strengthening us. It all comes together eventually.

I'm telling you here that your happiness is within, but within is also the place that we avoid going to the most. It is in that place where we hold the solutions, where we hold the ability and capacity to resolve our wounds. It's also in that place where we hold all the unresolved pain, maybe from our childhood or from relationship dynamics.

We also prefer to avoid feeling discomfort in our life. We hate feeling uncomfortable. So, what ends up happening is that we avoid the very place and space that holds all the answers. We build our coping mechanisms around this inner space within us by latching onto our outer space.

Inherited unhappiness

I've noticed that unhappiness is also a deep program that can stem from our DNA lineage. We can observe patterns of depression that have developed throughout life. There are cases of children born with depression, and the medical industry's only now waking up to it. That unhappiness and depression that are now coming forward is a predisposition.

We can also copy unhappiness behavior from a parent or caregiver we spent a lot of time with. Who in your life was always unhappy? Do you share any traits or patterns with that person? Something to think about. Sometimes our unhappiness does not belong to us.

Unhappiness can also psychosomatically show up in your body. I talk a lot about the psychosomatics of emotions, how we store them in the body, and how these patterns can control and manipulate certain ailments and its expressions. Remember, you are an expression of your ancestors. Everything that you're feeling and experiencing is a predisposition stemming from hundreds of years of accumulated experiences in your DNA lineage. A third of your life is being triggered and experienced by your ancestral memories, a third of your life!

Happiness depended on me

When is happiness going to come into my life? When am I going to wake up and just be happy? This was a big mistake I made, thinking happiness could come to me like a package being delivered from amazon.

There is no "one" specific way to be happy. There is no single key or a fixed formula we must follow to find true happiness. In fact, what works for one person may not work for everyone because happiness is deeply personal. Realizing that we have control over our happiness gives us a lot of power. While our family, friends, or loved ones are part of our "happiness team," they don't need to decide how we can be happy. The thing is, we handle our happiness whether we want to believe it or not.

After all, life throws up roadblocks that challenge everything we know about being happy. It sure as hell did for me. When everything seems to be turned upside-down and backward, it can be extremely difficult to fill our lives with happy vibes.

When you find yourself in the pit, hearing that happiness is a choice may be the last thing you want to hear. So, it's finding that spark, that light, that one thing you can cling to that will allow you to see the silver lining. Following that light, knowing happiness is a choice can make an enormous difference. Imagine sitting in an office, and you hate every minute. You don't want to be there. You feel so unhappy at that moment. You feel you must be there, and you are stuck feeling obligated. So, this is one scenario. It feels heavy, right? Now, I invite you to shift gears. Replay that scenario, but this time, you consciously decide that you chose to be there. You decided to get ready for work, and you sat in that chair and knocked out your work for the day. I invite you now to sit back for a few seconds and feel the difference. Which scenario feels lighter and more empowering? Do you get my message about the power of choice?

Happiness isn't a natural state of being (unless you are an infant and life hasn't really slapped you around), but a choice that we can all make every day. I want you to know that being genuinely happy does not mean a lack of negative emotions, such as sadness and pain. It is having the ability to be open to experiencing a wide range of emotions while appreciating - and remaining focused on - the positive aspects of life. It's a challenge to be happy, especially when life circumstances and situations are telling us otherwise.

Choosing to be happy requires constant effort, and to be honest, it does not come naturally. I've had to teach myself to think positively. I was a negative force. Indeed, like millions of others, I've dealt with periods of sadness and anxiety, even incidences of intrusive thoughts that have taken a toll on my happiness.

I've learned along the way that circumstances should not define my mood or dictate to me how to live my life. Happiness depends on me, as it is within me. It remains a choice, even if it takes focus and effort to stay positive, which it did for me. If anyone tells you they are always happy, then run.

I have learned that happiness also depends on my inherited predispositions. My parents had an unhealthy marriage. It was the principle of everything I didn't want in my future. My childhood upbringing also shaped my understanding of what happiness is. Then I spent the rest of my life trying to resolve my unhappiness and the programs behind it.

How much have you convinced yourself that you cannot have happiness in your life? There's a lot of cognitive mental programming taking place. There are a lot of neural pathways with cycles holding and formulating based on how you feel. It takes conscious effort to break these patterns. When we go against what we are used to, we feel resistance. What do you do when you feel resistance? Most of the time, you stop or divert away from the action you are taking. Moving towards happiness means you are going to move out of your routines and comfort zone. You will meet resistance at some point. How you move through that resistance will determine whether you are going to unleash that happiness within or stay as you are.

People who confront resistance are the ones who win in life. What is your relationship with resistance? If you hate it, then look at the attitude that you are bringing with you. It will magnify that resistance. Remember the example I shared with you about the office? If you choose to tackle resistance with a positive mindset, then resistance has no chance of ruining your flow in life.

Chapter 6

Fake or genuine happiness?

I've already touched on one of the greatest and biggest mistakes we make in life. We give too much power to relationship dynamics. This was true for me. I looked at the relationship dynamics and the environment I surrounded myself with. That includes all the material possessions that made me happy at that time.

One day I asked myself, how would I feel if I didn't have all these possessions in my life anymore? That is when the perceived happiness that I thought I had disappeared. It was a real "oh no" moment. It was a reality check. I realized I had painted a deluded picture for myself, thinking that I was happy, but the older I became, the more I lived my life, the more I realized that I knew nothing.

So much of my happiness depended on people, possessions, and circumstances. The bigger question I had for myself was, "what are the possessions and people allowing me to feel in my life that I cannot feel or have on my own?" The answer to this question changed my life and became the biggest healing journey that I had ever started. That became my biggest pursuit of rediscovering my real authentic happiness. I didn't realize that people, possessions, and circumstances were just covering up my shyness, low self-esteem, and lack of confidence in my talents.

My identity was so connected to people in these circumstances that I lost my sense of self. I lost my connection with myself to the point where I had to ask myself, if I didn't have all these things in my life, what would make me happy? God, the saddest question that came from that was, "who am I?"

Who am I if I don't have all these things? I was once sitting in a group I didn't know. We were talking about happiness. We were all sharing life stories. We went around the table and we all just shared. We all had to share a significant moment in our life. I shared there too, and my focus was on accomplishments such as possessions and so forth. That was part of my realization. I realized that money, people, circumstances, possessions, and material things owned me. They absolutely owned me.

What was interesting is that in my childhood, I've had everything, and I've also had absolutely nothing. We had everything. My father had a business worth millions, and he failed due to his alcoholism and poor decisions. My mother and I briefly ended up in a caravan park when in winter, which it was at the time, the water pipes were frozen, and you couldn't brush your teeth because you didn't have running water. Then after that, we landed ourselves in the worst neighborhood. The first day we moved into a small house, our neighbors broke out in a gunshot fight over drugs.

I've had both spectrums. You would think that by having that you would grow up humbler. You would grow up with a better understanding of what happiness is once you've truly had nothing. It's almost like there's a part of me that worked so hard to get happiness back because I realized I associated happiness with what I had. Why? Because I was so damn unhappy when I didn't have everything and that is when I associated possessions and money with happiness.

I associated happiness with what I had, and my highest value was financial security because the trauma of losing it was so great. I built my entire life around rebuilding that financial security. I was rebuilding it, and I was just 29 years old and a self-made millionaire as well as a business owner. Back then, in the early 2000s date range, that was an accomplishment and a half.

The funny thing was three years later, I walked away from it all. I walked away from everything because it was toxic happiness. Did I overcompensate by walking away from it? Absolutely! Was it worth it when I looked back? Yes, it was. I know what it's like to fall flat on your face, but I also know what it's like to rise again. I knew the steps. This knowledge was my strength.

I ended up in Bali in a local compound, saving every penny after a divorce. I had to rebuild my life back up again from scratch, which I did. I was a bit of an extremist back in the day, and I don't regret it one bit. That fight and push I had, especially when I came face to face with resistance, was my saving grace.

I truly had to ask myself if I had let go of all the artificial happiness, would I really be able to find true happiness? The shock of losing what I created and the false happiness it brought me was intense. Once you let go, it gets easier. I always tell my students that staying in a challenging situation is hard, but it can't be harder than taking a step that can set you free in the long term.

Sometimes, you need to just rip off that band-aid and take a small step in the right direction. Steps you take toward your inner happiness do not have to be dramatic or traumatic. It can be a gradual and gentle process. Remember to choose it.

You can gradually come to realize where you are at in your life. You can assess where you need to make changes in your life. If I didn't have all this experience and hadn't gone through these events, I wouldn't be here with you, sharing this life experience so that you can choose your next best step forward. What are my options? This is the beauty of sharing our life experiences.

I like to think of happiness like classical music that plays in the background all the time. It's like a state of being. It's always there in the background. Sometimes you will have intense emotions coming forward, and you will not hear that classical music in the background. So, once your intense emotions settle down, you hear the music again. When you can return to your happiness and have an awareness of its presence, that is when inner happiness has been uncovered. This is my way of interpreting it and it does not have to be yours.

Happiness is part of your identity

What if you don't like who you are? Does that mean you can't find happiness? This can be challenging. It's hard to separate the two. I hated who I was. My father's constant toxic feedback messed up my perception of myself. His feedback became my truth and what I thought of myself. Imagine this. If your identity was abused, attacked, or rejected, you might end up rejecting your own identity. No one enjoys being connected to something that makes them feel bad, that can even include your relationship with yourself. That was me in a nutshell.

Have you considered the possibility that perhaps how you were treated in the past became your relationship with yourself? That feedback influences the barometer by which we measure our self-worth. We then spend the rest of our lives trying to delete that feedback so that we can return to our authentic selves.

The very thing, such as my happiness and mindset around it, felt rejected. I had made a negative association with my identity. How I projected my identity resulted in me being abused. I was a cheerful kid. My father hated that. He hated it when someone was happy while he was in a depressed state, which he was always in.

He beat that happiness right out of me. I grew up in a childhood that I call the crayfish in a pot syndrome. Sadly, this was because of my father. He was very good at free diving for crayfish with a snorkel. He would go down into the rocks, 20 meters below, and grab these crayfish, catching them to cook in a pot.

Sadly, he would put them in a boiling pot alive, and that's how he would cook them. What you would see these crayfish do is try to get out. If one crayfish is almost successful in getting out, it would be pulled back by the first of the crayfish in the pot instead of thinking, oh, perfect, I can climb out of the pot over you, but it pulls it back in.

At least, that's how I perceived it as a child. It's a great analogy, because sometimes there are some households with certain family dynamics that have crayfish in them. They have one person upset, especially the leader or the alpha male or the alpha female. If they're upset, God forbid you are happy at that moment.

I'm talking back to the seventies and eighties. When it was still that old school program that kids should be seen and not heard. I'm sure it's still happening today, but I'm seeing new parents in the new age breaking that cycle.

Do you associate happiness with happiness?

Let me ask you this instead. Imagine when you feel happy, and someone punishes you at that same moment. Instead of feeling happy, you will be upset, and if you notice your emotional response to the punishment. You will see that a new negative emotion replaced your happiness. One incident can be enough to anchor this in your mind as a traumatic event. This means, consciously or subconsciously, the memory of this moment will remain in your psyche. When you feel happy again, what can happen? It can trigger the memory of punishment, triggering with it how you felt in that moment. So instead of remembering what happiness feels like, you remember the emotional aftermath of the punishment you experienced.

You associate a positive experience with the traumatic aftermath. We then associate happiness with something that is unsafe. It is an excellent example of how we form traumatic memories around something that is a positive experience.

So, it meant something was supposed to be positive, especially if you had a positive association with happiness, and happiness came to you easily. Maybe when you were a kid, you felt happy. There may have been a traumatic event that overshadowed the happiness you felt. That event and your emotional response to it can become a happiness block.

This old wound is being continuously triggered in your subconscious mind by your environment. This is an example I use when I explain unhappiness and a block behind it. When you have a thought such as I want to be happy. It's a conscious thought. What do we do? We think of positive ways that we can create it.

We don't sit there thinking, how can I ruin this? How much can I sabotage my happiness right now? We don't do that. However, you subconsciously project that positive thought, such as I want to be happy, but what happens when you have trauma associated with the very thing that we want?

Your emotions remember what this stress felt like. Your subconscious mind remembers, too. You might feel anxious. Maybe you just feel like hiding or, you feel suddenly unworthy, or shame is being triggered, but you do not know why. You have a subconscious memory that is being triggered and your body is showing you an old emotional reaction to it.

Your subconscious mind will now respond to your thought, "Oh, you want the happiness, perfect. Let's go look in the subconscious mind at previous memories that we have stored that are associated with happiness. Hmm? Oh, do you remember that time when your father hit you when you were happy? Or when you showed him the exam results you thought were fantastic, but he thought you did terrible, and you got punished?" What is going to take place now? Your body will have a biochemical reaction to the negative memory associated with feeling happy. Have you ever thought of this possibility as a being a happiness block?

Happiness when life is hard

Oh, this is tough. How can we be happy when we're having difficult times or when we know that the surrounding people are miserable? It's easy to enjoy life and be happy when things are going well. During trying times, you can attempt to pay attention to what makes you happy and use that as a bridge to face and overcome your hurdles. How can you choose to be happy when you're surrounded by pain and frustration? Repetition helped me.

I would repeat the positive thought, "I want happiness," because, in order for you to think that you deserve happiness in a moment of turmoil, repetition helps. We must keep on reinforcing it. It's not like we can just decide, "oh, I want to be happy now." The feeling of happiness might not last long. You might even feel it for just one minute before a negative memory possibly associated with happiness pops up and ruins your moment.

What happens, then? The body biochemically starts a new cycle again, triggering negative memories associated with happiness.

Small things that helped me

Happiness does not depend on our current life situation or stressors. It's not a fleeting thing we experience when our stars align, and our life is problem-free. Sometimes, we can choose to be intentional about being happy.

Even in the face of hardships like work challenges, family problems, tragedy, or even life-threatening diagnosis, you can empower yourself and others to be happy. For instance, by engaging in specific "feel good" activities, we can increase our natural happiness set points. You can try to include these activities to help create happy vibes during tough times.

Take care of yourself: Do you feel good after going to the gym or getting a haircut? Sometimes, having a lengthy bath, getting your nails done, or wearing your favorite sneakers can put you in a good mood. Simply paying attention to your mind and body can significantly affect your mental health.

These are fast ways to experience joy:

- Play your favorite music: Listening to your favorite jams provides an escape from the day-to-day difficulties you may be facing. It can naturally give your mood a boost while studying, reading a book, or just hanging out. You can even play and sing along to your favorite tunes, as it can reduce your anxiety and help improve your sleep quality, too. Binary beats are legit!

- Focus on small moments in the present: When you feel overwhelmed, it's best to take life one day at a time. Whether this means having coffee with a good friend, playing online games, or painting, do something that sparks joy. When you take time each day to do something that you love, difficult periods can seem more manageable, and being happy becomes a lot more natural. I like to think back to things that made me smile.

- Indulge your senses: You might not be aware of this, but anything, taste, smell, hearing, or touch can affect your mood.

For instance, does seeing a butterfly or spraying perfume make you feel excited? So, take a moment to do something that will awaken your senses and bring a happy vibe. It can be from satisfying your sweet tooth, watching feel-good series, or lighting a scented candle. Aromatherapy can be like having a therapist without the bill!

- Unleash your inner child: Growing up comes with rigidness that we lose sight of our inner child. Bring back that inner spirit you once have so you can truly enjoy life and experience happiness. I'm certain that getting silly, riding a roller coaster, having a sleepover with friends, or rolling down the grassy hill can bring that pure bliss.

- Change your routine: Doing the same thing repeatedly can make you feel stuck in a rut! Do you always go to class without taking breakfast or sleep late at night? Why not try to start your day with a healthy breakfast and sleep earlier than usual? Giving your daily routine a shake and even trying new things allows you to experience unexpected joy and excitement.

- Give yourself a treat: It's not harmful to treat yourself if you're going through a difficult time. This doesn't have to break your allowance. So, if you feel like buying a new outfit or taking yourself out to a movie, then give yourself the experience you dream of having. Let those things spark joy.

- Extend a helping hand: It's important to look after yourself but being there for others can also brighten your mood. This doesn't even have to cost you a lot or take too much of your time. For instance, you can simply smile at your elderly neighbors or support local businesses that are struggling. Helping others the way you can lift your spirits in ways you may not realize was possible.

Chapter 7

The Stepping Exercise

I hope that you're putting one and one together because it's really, really, really super important. So, let's do an exercise. I feel on a biological level, it's so deeply important, especially today, with all the disconnection that we have. First, let's understand why most of us avoid self-connection.

How many times did you scroll through your social media feeds today? How long did you play games or watch Netflix shows? Which of those activities pique your curiosity?

We live in a busy, tumultuous world which makes it easier to ignore ourselves and our feelings. With Facebook, Instagram, TikTok, Twitter, YouTube, and messages from your Messenger all competing for your attention 24-hours a day, we get lost in our daily activities and the stress that the world brings. We choose to focus almost always on anything and anyone but ourselves.

Every second you spend on mindless interactions deprives you of connecting with yourself and your energy, that could be channeled to a better place.

Instead of appreciating yourself and acknowledging what you have, you get into the comparison trap. Social media can make you feel you're competing with others, judging yourself based on other people's lives and what they have. This may even make you feel like racing with everyone else instead of living within your timeline.

We constantly desire to please those around us, thinking that through this, we can get the appreciation, respect, and happiness we are looking for. We probably struggle with fear and worry that we'll get to uncover once we get to see our true selves. Because of this, we ignore the very need to reconnect with ourselves.

When you can't connect with your true self, everything can turn into a stressful and frustrating game. Most of the time, we feel stuck, unsupported, or depressed because we choose to ignore ourselves.

What makes us happy isn't about what we have or how people perceive it. It's about who we truly are and how we live our lives. That's valuable because people cannot take that away from you. One great thing about self-connection is being able to listen to yourself and your needs. To live a fulfilling and happy life, it's vital that you know, connect, and fall in love with yourself.

Learning to connect with yourself allows you to better understand what makes you tick and allows you to tap into all of life's potential. When you embrace the relationship, you have with yourself, every other connection that you have will grow.

Let me tell you that doing mindfulness practices can make you feel more connected with yourself. This gives you a way to better understand what makes you tick and tap into your potential. When you value the relationship you have with yourself, everything else follows.

It's only right that you give yourself the same gentle, loving care that you are giving to those you care about the most. I promise that investing in getting to know yourself will make an enormous difference in how you view happiness.

When I did this, I experienced a renewed zest for life because I am more connected to my feelings, needs, goals, and dreams. The stepping exercise is fantastic. It helps you to subconsciously, gracefully, and safely, connect to sensations and emotions. Maybe even fears, thoughts, and patterns that you might feel really stuck with.

Sensations that might be felt during this exercise are held in the emotional body, not just cognitively held in our mind, but throughout the emotional body. A lot of you might know about my research. We're going to connect to the part of you that is happy.

For this exercise, I invite you to pretend that you are happy. You are going to imagine a version for you that is 100% happy in life.

So, what you'll do is to stand up with an open space in front of you at least two meters or six feet.

At the end of these two meters or six feet, you are now going to pretend that you can either hear, feel, see, or sense a copy of you that is 100% happy in life.

What would you look like?

What would you feel like?

What would you sound like if you truly had your happiness?

What would it feel like if you had all your needs met?

Now, slowly, slowly, slowly, walk towards that part of you. As slowly as possible and you're going to feel emotions coming up. If you feel frozen, step into that feeling. Continue to step into whichever emotion arises until you get to the end. Until you reach the happy version of yourself. Once you do, step into that version of yourself and merge with it.

This process is going to reveal many aspects of yourself. I would highly recommend that you journal your experience when you are done. I have very important questions to ask you once you are done with your exercise.

Question 1: What were your five most dominant reactions during the exercise?

Question 2: What do you need to let go of in order to become fully happy?

Question 3: What do you need to accept about yourself so that your light can shine?

What are you going to do with the answers to these questions? You see, knowledge is power however, that power is useless if it's not acted on. The ball is now in your court.

If you feel a block, then you can always head over to my recorded session www.guidedhealingsession.com it's in our free MAT Membership site under courses.

Chapter 8

Finding and achieving balance

Remember that happiness means different things for all of us, and the same goes for other people. For some, they are pursuing the goals that they expect will bring them happiness. So, happiness isn't always the result. Some successful people put everything into their careers at the expense of their health and personal lives, only to wonder why they are still unhappy. It's also too common for people to be surrounded by fame, money, designer clothes, and expensive cars and still feel unsatisfied and miserable in their lives.

Now, try to imagine a life where you consciously had meaningful relationships with family and friends, did things you love, and looked forward to going to class and learning something every day. You purposefully eat healthily and exercise in ways that make you happy. You choose to be active and live a spiritual life. You even enjoy wearing the same set of clothes or the same shoes repeatedly, because that's what you're comfortable in.

This means that when you have prioritized balance, you are exuding self-respect in every aspect of your life, especially towards yourself. The unpleasant things in life don't stress you. The very things that are hard to control now seem to be bearable. The idea behind this is that you can create a life of balance. Having a balanced life means a balance of mind, body, and emotions. When you find peace and comfort in what you are doing, and in your circumstances, you become happier, and you experience self-love.

When we have too much of one thing, it can lead to anxiety, stress, and even feelings of isolation and resentment. For instance, if you only care about getting that ideal job, you might sacrifice your health and your time with your family and friends. Or if you spend all your time and energy on your social life or activities, you might neglect your relationship responsibilities.

The thing here is that finding a balance that works for you can pave the way to fulfillment and happiness in all aspects of your life. All these moments start with mindfulness. Take a moment to think about this. What is something that you want to do and enjoy doing? Does it bring balance to your life?

Every aspect of your life - your work responsibilities, personal life, relationships, health, and other meaningful pursuits plays a role in your happiness. Don't simply devote all your time and energy to pursuing a single thing. You neglect every other aspect of your life. Here's the truth: Happiness isn't a quick fix, but a balancing act. To experience true, lasting happiness, you need to find and achieve balance.

It all comes down to understanding that happiness and sadness exist together. Mastering happiness doesn't mean that you will be happy all the time and you will experience beautiful, incredible moments all the time. Rainstorms will remain to be part of your life, and you will continue to go through them in your journey.

Being able to see happiness gives you power over the sad moments as you treasure those happy moments. You realize that when you get dampened by the rain or feel the warmth of the sun on your face, everything remains to be part of the ebb and flow of life.

All those circumstances bring about the balance of life. You will not try to chase being happy or ignore those negative experiences. Instead, you will learn to grow and find meaning in all those positive and negative experiences. In the end, you will see them as meaningful experiences that will help you grow and achieve fulfillment. That's the time you'll know the value and live the true meaning of happiness.

The role of gratitude in your happiness

This really worked for me. When things are tough, it's hard to feel grateful. The path towards lasting happiness doesn't just happen by chance. Still, there are things you can do that will put you on the track to a life filled with happiness and fulfillment! It starts by developing an attitude of gratitude for everything happening around us. This allows us to be fully present in every moment and enjoy life.

Giving thanks for what you have is one of the simplest and most powerful ways to boost happiness and increase feelings of gratitude. When we take the time to reflect on the things that we are thankful for, whether it be our friends, our family, our health, or anything else, it helps us to shift our focus away from our problems and onto the things that matter.

By fostering a positive attitude of gratitude, we can appreciate all the good things happening in our lives. Whether it is simply savoring a delicious meal or soaking up the sun on a warm summer day, this mindset allows us to be fully present and savor each experience until it passes. This perspective also helps us to see challenges as opportunities for growth and happiness rather than as obstacles that bring only frustration and despair. With an attitude of gratitude, we can truly embrace all that life offers and live each day to the fullest.

Gratitude opens our hearts and helps us to feel more connected with others. When we feel more connected, we experience true happiness and greater satisfaction.

Keep in mind that it is our attitude of thankfulness that enables us to experience and appreciate each moment completely. When we express gratitude, we open ourselves up to receiving more blessings and to experiencing true happiness.

Thus, it's essential to find things to be thankful for in our lives, no matter how big or small. By practicing gratitude, we can shift our focus from negative to positive and start attracting better things into our lives. Also, in today's hectic world, it is easy to get caught up in the hustle and bustle of daily life. Between busy schedules, endless to-do lists, and constant distractions from technology, it can feel like we are never present in the moment or fully appreciating our lives.

By cultivating an attitude of gratitude, we can slow down, be truly mindful of each moment, and embrace happiness as a natural part of life. By staying attuned to what is around us, we can truly experience all that life offers. Let me share this with you. Being thankful serves to make me feel better. When I feel grateful, my mind focuses on all those blessings that make up who I truly am. This allows me to savor my experiences more fully, which ultimately improves both my mental health and physical well-being.

The key here is learning what makes us happy and then letting that lead our way forward, no matter how much stuff tries to pull us away from happiness (like stress or anxiety).

Gratitude unlocks the fullness of our lives. It makes everything seem better and more fulfilling and this can include relationships with family members to mundane tasks such as getting up in the morning or taking a shower. It's what leads us through happy moments that are simple yet profound.

It is an essential key for unlocking the happiness that we have within ourselves. When we're feeling grateful, our mind strives towards good things happening around us because they know how much effort was placed into making those things happen! Since gratitude is a state of mind that can be cultivated through practice, you can start activating gratitude in your routine.

Ways to cultivate gratitude

We all express gratitude in several ways. We can do so by applying it to our past, present, and even future experiences. The first step is to find things in your life to be grateful for. This could be something as simple as a roof over your head or being able to see the sunrise each morning. When you focus on the good things in your life, it becomes easier to let go of the negative thoughts that can keep happiness at bay.

- Keep a gratitude journal: Every day, write three things you're grateful for. This can be anything from your bed to a great cup of coffee.
- Give thanks before meals: Before you eat, take a moment to say thanks for the food. You can even bless the meal if you like.
- Show appreciation: Whenever someone does something nice for you, let them know how much you appreciate it. A simple "thank you" goes a long way.

- Pay it forward: When someone does something kind for you, try to do the same for someone else. This creates a chain reaction of positivity and happiness.

- Write a Thank You note: Nurture your relationships by expressing your appreciation to people around you. Make it a habit to send someone a gratitude message, and don't forget to write one for yourself, too.

- Count your blessings: No matter how busy you are, always find time to reflect on the things you are grateful for. You can start by writing one to three things that you can connect with. As you do this, feel the sensation that it has provided you with.

- Say affirmations: You can say affirmations of gratitude out loud or in your head throughout the day. Repeating positive statements about what you're grateful for will help train your mind to focus on the good in your life.

- Do random acts of kindness: It could be something as simple as letting someone go ahead of you in line or paying for the coffee of the person behind you in line. These slight gestures can make a big difference in someone else's day, and they can also help increase your happiness.

- Have minutes of reflection: Simply take a few moments each day to reflect on the good in your life (even if some things aren't going well) and savor the happy memories you've made.

The best way to cultivate a gratitude habit is not to wait for special moments. You simply have to be more mindful even of little things happening in your life - from the warm cup of tea you are enjoying to the pizza delivery guy who makes sure that your orders arrive on time.

Being grateful allows us to focus on what we have, rather than always looking for new things and hoping it will make us happier. It helps us refocus our minds on what we have instead of what we lack. While we may initially feel contrived, consistent practice makes it easier and more powerful.

One of the best things about gratitude is that it's free! You need nothing except a positive attitude to get started. The more you become grateful - through reminding yourself of all the things that make your life great or by showing gratitude to those around you - the happier you will feel.

So, whatever you're doing right now - take a moment to pause and reflect on all the happiness that surrounds you. After all, there's no better way to enjoy your journey than by living in the present with an attitude of gratitude. When you feel down next time you're, try practicing gratitude and see how it affects your mood. This simple habit can make a big difference in your life and the lives of those around you.

Chapter 9

Stop trying to be happy

I know we all want to be happy all the time. It's natural, but it should not be the goal. What your idea of happiness at this moment will differ from what you want it to be in the future.

To feel true happiness, there are two things that we need to do. One is to stop chasing happiness, and the next is not to make happiness the goal. This may sound counterintuitive, right? When we chase something, it will only make us more anxious, stressed out, and unhappy.

The thing is, we grew up thinking that a perfect life means happiness. We assume people who have perfect lives are happy all the time. We are conditioned with the idea of "happily-ever-after." That fairytale books and movies give us. We correlate happiness with what we see on social media, where everyone shares the best aspects of their lives. This will only distort how we view happiness.

The reality is that no one is living a perfect life. It doesn't exist. Even the wealthiest billionaires and famous people have their own share of countless problems, miseries, and downfalls. What we can do is to embrace that happiness is a fluctuation of positive and negative moments. Instead of focusing on the darkness, find reasons for how you can be grateful for the light. You don't have to push those negative emotions and cover them up with artificial joy, as you'll only end up hurting yourself.

Keep in mind if you really want to be happy, think of happiness as something that happens. We don't have to achieve it or chase it, as it isn't something to be found. We can't even uncover it by sacrificing our time, health, and well-being. Happiness is a never-ending process we experience, something that we build up every day based on what we care about.

Understand that you have the capacity to choose what to do with your life and transform what you feel about it. Most of the time, by simply allowing yourself to be in the moment, happiness will flow naturally for you.

Remember that your attitude reflects happiness. Cultivating an optimistic mind leads to cultivating happiness, no matter what your circumstances are. This also means making it a habit to appreciate yourself and those around you. Your attitude about life and everything that happens to you each day creates a tremendous impact on your satisfaction, fulfillment, and overall happiness.

Still, we are all different, and I know that not all these work for each of us. Reaching your greatest potential and finding fulfillment depends on you alone.

When you look for lessons in every situation, you will get to take full control of your conscious mind. You'll get to view the world in a brighter, more optimistic way. Looking for the good in others and seeing the world the way you want it to be can make an enormous difference in how you will feel.

Know that you can create happiness and make the most out of it. When you discover and commit to your purpose in life and listen to your heart, you will gain fullness and meaning in all aspects of your life. Happiness is natural and is always there.

Choosing happiness also sometimes means getting rid of toxic influences that stand in the way of your happiness. Instead of setting unrealistic expectations, make your happiness easy to grasp. Know that sharing joy with others is more rewarding than chasing your happiness.

We can think of happiness as a signal that we are living our life in accordance with what we care about. We should be mindful not to lose sight of what the world is trying to tell us. Happiness can be felt in the simplest brief moments that make life worth living. It all boils down to realizing that we can value the process and this entire journey.

Happiness is something you become and it's something that you already are. When we stop chasing and pursuing it, we realize happiness has been right in front of us all along. As happiness comes in many forms, embrace one that speaks and matters to you the most - and hold on to that.

Now, take time to breathe and relax. Let go trying to please people. What about you? Feel happiness like a gentle stream that's flowing within you.

Find the core that makes you feel at peace and makes your heart smile. When you feel better, you find that the world around you feels a lot better, too. The moment you choose to look around and within you, I'm certain that you'll feel what truly makes you happy.

Final thoughts

Keep in mind that happiness is living a life that brings you joy, purpose, and fulfillment. You need nothing else and you don't have to wait to be happy. Mastering happiness is a continuous journey, and it starts with small steps and thoughts that will make you feel happy with yourself. You can choose to be happy right now and take steps to feel better each day.

We see happiness as our goal in life, for we think that once we achieve what we desire, that's the time that we'll be happy. Sometimes, when we reach that point, the feelings that we have are only short-lived and it leads us back into the endless cycle of pursuit and disappointment. As we keep on chasing, we get overwhelmed and never stop questioning ourselves whether we are flawed, inadequate, or simply undeserving. Life remains complex and uncertain, and you don't need to force happiness every moment of every day. It is only when you shift your perspective on happiness and what it means to be happy that you notice more.

Happiness results from knowing and fulfilling your purpose. Are you certain about what you want to do and your purpose in life? Figuring out and understanding the very reason for your existence is one that gives you the most satisfaction and fulfillment. This gives you full ownership of your life, allows you to sleep better, practice healthy habits, have strong relationships, and have better mental health. When you figure it out, you'll experience a greater sense of well-being and fulfillment, and happiness will be there, tagging along with you.

Affirmations

I deserve to be happy because I said so.

It is my right to be happy because no one else holds that right.

I am worthy as I am.

I am happy with who I am because that is my choice.

I am loved and accepted just as I am, hell yeah, I am.

I release all negative thoughts about myself. I am no longer listening.

I am free to be myself because I was born free.

I forgive myself for all my past mistakes.

I now choose to focus on the positive aspects of my life because I am an optimistic fairy.

I am grateful for all the good things in my life. I allow myself to receive more of what I want.

I choose to be happy from this moment on and that decision is final.

About the Author

Evette Rose is an Author, Life Coach, Metaphysical Anatomy Technique (M.A.T) development company and founder of several books. Evette was born in South Africa and grew up in Namibia, West Africa. She then moved to Australia, lived in Vanuatu and Bali. She is best known for her work in helping people to resolve trauma from their past and freeing them to live successful and fulfilling lives. Evette's work is drawn from her own personal

experience of moving from a difficult past into a well-balanced life and career. Evette's philosophy is that we, as a human race, are not destined to live our lives in pain because of past trauma or abuse. We often suppress our ability to complete or heal trauma naturally. In today's society, we often suppress our pain in order to keep up with life and avoid being left behind. Fortunately, through gentle therapy, this natural internal healing instinct can be restored. Writing her books has helped Evette reach out to other people who need love, support, and someone to relate to. She shares her experiences with the world, hoping it will help people heal and provide encouragement and reassurance when they need it most. Evette now travels the world teaching personal development seminars and continues her research journey. She has been to well over 40 countries and worked with thousands of people!

References

https://www.stylesalute.com/key-to-happiness-laws-of-attraction/

https://iaap-journals.onlinelibrary.wiley.com/doi/full/10.1111/aphw.12200

https://www.psychalive.org/how-to-use-tough-times-for-truly-connecting-to-yourself/

https://www.helpguide.org/articles/healthy-living/finding-joy-during-difficult-times.htm

https://www.betterhelp.com/advice/happiness/happiness-is-a-choice-how-to-be-happy/

Metaphysical Anatomy Technique Volume 2

Printed in Great Britain
by Amazon

46137873R00056